AF674435

Good Manners

Be Kind And Polite

Om KIDZ

An imprint of Om Books International

Kindness and politeness are two of the greatest qualities that are sadly lacking in most of us today.

Remember, your behaviour and manners reveal your true character! Being kind and polite will ensure that you are listening to other people's views on a problem before you find a solution.

This will make your relationship with people much better. Not to mention that you will be a better human being and always at peace. So go ahead and make the first move!

Open the door for people you don't know, sacrifice your last brownie for your younger brother or sister, compliment your friend about his new haircut and buy your mother some flowers.

Be kind and polite, not only to your friends and relatives, but also to people you don't know.

An act of kindness can go a long way. If you are travelling by public transport and it is crowded, always offer your seat to an elderly person.

Help an old person cross the street or volunteer to help carry their bags! It is important to be kind and polite to people from all walks of life. If you manage to do that successfully, you will be loved and respected by everyone.

Being kind and polite is the most important thing to learn as far as good manners are concerned. There might be times when you find it difficult to control your anger, but being polite in all situations is the best solution.

You should treat everyone with kindness and politeness, even the ones who may not have learnt politeness. Remember, they might be impolite, but you must remain civil as it reflects on who you are.

When you speak to people, never raise your voice, even if they do so. Remaining calm is one of the most important steps towards being kind and polite.

Being kind and polite doesn't cost a cent. All you need is good manners, common sense and a genuine feeling of love and humanity for others to build harmony.

Smile when you are introduced to someone. Be friendly, helpful and sensitive to other people's feelings. Make sure you greet people when you meet them.

You don't have to follow all the suggestions in order to be kind and polite. It is important to just be yourself and not be too uptight with the rules of kindness and politeness.

The need to be polite has to come from deep within you and remember that there is no such thing as 'too kind' or 'too polite'.

Wise men have rightly said that the secret to happiness truly lies in being kind and polite to fellow human beings!